Unspoken

Sydney Moss

BookLeaf
Publishing

India | USA | UK

Presentation by *BookLeaf Publishing*

Web: www.bookleafpub.com

E-mail: info@bookleafpub.com

ISBN: 9789357446914

First edition 2022

DEDICATION

I would like to dedicate this book to everyone who has encouraged me to keep writing, and to everyone who has inspired me no matter the light of the situation. I have learned from all of you, good and bad, and I thank you for the individual experiences you have gifted me. Specifically I am dedicating this anthology to my parents, for teaching me to be a self-aware and critical thinker, to Brady for being the best example of how writing is not a one-size-fits-all phenomenon but rather a world wide source of expression and communication despite differences, and to Charlee Kate for reminding me why I write, why any of us write: for the future; may you learn from our mistakes and chase after the want for a better world with the awareness of our brokenness and the mistakes of generations before you while finding comfort in our words knowing that we've been through it too. Lastly I dedicate this book to Mat, you encourage me daily and love me so well. Thank you all.

ACKNOWLEDGEMENT

This truly would not have been possible if it weren't for the many people who have helped me write the story of my life, every person that I've known for a sentence, a paragraph, a chapter... a book. I have been inspired by so many of you and I thank you for that, wherever you are.

PREFACE

Just like any piece of literary work, the following anthology is entirely up for interpretation- the main goal is to awaken something within anyone who so generously chooses to read what I've written. No matter where you are in life, I hope there is something in here that speaks to you, or perhaps that it makes you feel a little less alone and a little more seen. There are so many things not being talked about, but I promise I've thought what you're thinking, and that if I haven't somebody has, we all have a story that we only tell part of. I hope this anthology encourages you to tell more of yours.

Please Don't Let Go

People ask why it makes sense to me
To mourn the loss of another tree
Another tree, a broken bell
A little old woman who tripped and fell
Why do you mourn those whom you don't
know?
Why so sad about the ringing bell?
One less bell, one less tree
What does it matter?
It matters to me.
Some day when I am reduced to dust
Stripped of all my wanderlust
When the world has no more use for me
And uses my body to nourish a tree
I hope someone would mourn for me
Mourn for me and love the tree
Remember my voice as the toll of the bell
My absence will acquaint you with silence well

So next time you see me weep
For the willow, maple or oak
Or for the little old woman who never awoke
Or for the bell
Whose chimes are reduced to a choke
Remember I'm mourning so much more

Than a stranger, a bell, or a tree no one knew
well
I weep for the loss of a life lined with laughter
And pain, and sorrow
Someone who will not know tomorrow
I weep for the weighted silence
In place of the toll of the regal bell
I weep for a noble, tall and sturdy tree
Giver of life and shelter
And beauty for my eyes to see
I would hope you feel the same for me

And when my time on earth has come and gone
I hope there's someone
Who will choose to hold on
To compassion and love and those who are lost
Hold on for me, hold on for the tree
Hold on for the bell
And for the little old woman who tripped and
fell.

Empty Cups

You say that it hurts to be kind
That the love you give leaves you drained
And broken inside
I have news for you my friend
It's not the giving or the helping
Or the loving
It's part you
And part who you're giving to
It's the way you give with the expectation to
receive
Oh, when will you learn
To play the game?
People aren't givers, not even close
Not even lovers, or feelers
Empathy's ghost

The sooner you learn that
The safer you'll be
I promise, I promise
Take it from me

So does this mean that people don't need love?
Certainly not
Far from it, my dove
People need love like the air that they breathe

They look to the world
They can't find it or make it
So they take it from you
And from me
And it's all we can do
To offer it up
The little love droplets from the depths of our
cups

But how much nicer would it be to give from a
cup which is full?
Nicer, maybe
Easier, indeed
But even those with cups half-full find ways to
be free
It's not the size of your cup
Or really even how much is in it
But what, what do you fill it with?

Fill your cup with love and praise
And those things will flow from you for all of
your days
But a cup full of pity
Is doomed to decay
And destined to rust
It will weather, dry out
And collect mounds of dust
So find the people down on their luck
Rise from your slump

And put a little love in their cup

5

The Hunter, The Clock

Isn't it funny?
We try so hard to preserve every memory
Pictures and artifacts, inanimate objects
To try and remember living things
Living people
But no matter how many things we write down
Or how many pictures we take
No matter how many of their hats and shirts
We keep to hold at night
Our memories fail us and fade and weather
All of the written words we read
Feel as if they came from a stranger
Someone else's love story, struggles or triumphs
So why do we try to remember the things we
know we'll forget in time?
Because people like to try
We are an entire population of individuals
Fighting mortality and memory loss
So go on collecting your artifacts
And clinging to the bits of life you write down
That's what I'll do
I'll go on pretending that life isn't short

I'll go on pretending that time is capable of
standing still
Even though all it's really doing is passing by
The hands of the clock haunting and hunting
each of us down

Liar, Liar

I write and I write and I write
And I read and I read and I read
Someone it seems has planted a seed
"And I have so many thoughts!"
I say as a plea
But not one of you cares to hear them
This is what I see, what I see
I have thoughts of good and thoughts of bad
So you call me a hypocrite
A writer gone mad

When did we lose the right
To have both joy and grievance with life?
I'm tired and grateful
And loving and hateful
God himself knows
We exist juxtaposed
Everyone feels as if nobody knows
Nobody feels
"Nobody feels what I feel"
But we do, you're not special
Whether you're high, or you're low
Somebody knows
So wipe your crocodile tears
Hide your fears

And join the rest of the pretenders and menders
Who would much rather feel like they have
something to say
Than to actually say it
At the end of the day
You are one of them
And so am I
We're all just looking for truth
In the lies.

Morality Unhinged

Another one?
Another what?
Another Shooting?
Oh, that
It's all part of their plan
Whose plan? Who would plan this?
Why on earth would anyone plan this?
Have we lost sight of all that matters?
Why are we fighting over the color of his skin?
Someone is dead, his life cut short
No matter what 'agenda' you say this is a part of
No matter how many posts you make about
blatant injustice
The greater battle is being lost behind your
backs
We grow apart, further divided now
At war with one side or another
Or within ourselves
This is all so wrong
This is not how it's supposed to be
But then again
When was the last time
You saw someone act
As they should?

The Prison of Icarus

Icarus, the story we hear of a boy
Raised in a maze
Who dreamed of escape
Of a better tomorrow
And when granted the chance to fly
Flew into the sun
And laughed as he died
Used as a lesson in moderation
But don't we forget?
He was somebody's son
And I know we all shake our heads in pity
This tragedy of impiety
But how lucky each of us would be
To be as recklessly free
As icarus
It could be argued that his wings were his prison
But how wrong that would be
His prison is my own, and yours as well
It is mortality
Icarus simply didn't care
His taste of freedom lit a fire in him
Before it lit a fire on him
His embrace of freedom was unbridled and pure
And we are all so safe that we could never know
for sure

What freedom feels like to the caged
To those victim to where they were raised
If you believe Icarus is a lesson in moderation
I beg of you a simple question
What would you do, and who would you be
If after years in a maze
You were granted a chance to be free?
To Icarus, every day was the same
So this new feeling of freedom left him amazed
Doomed by his own sheltering, he soared
But how could he have known?
Dear Icarus there was so much more
But thank you for showing us the power of
freedom
And the dangers of its absence
Your story is relevant and awakening
In past, present, future tense

The Maker

So here we are
Another year into this deep, darkening hole
We got ourselves into
We see a villain and a hero atop a hill
Wielding different weapons created by the same
maker
Chants and cheers and slurs all mix together
As much discrepancy between the praise and
ridicule
As there is between grass and weeds

The world has never known such turmoil
Yet at the same time
Nothing has changed
It's always been this way

People of a nation who believe it is indeed
United we stand
Divide into sides, neither having a clear glimpse
Of what is truly good
And neither accepting that they could ever be
bad
Only knowing that the other side
Surely must be

We stand on a mountain made of fallen soldiers
Who fought not for good or bad but for the truth
We rest in beds of lies from which we will never
awake
To see the mistakes of our kind
Pride divides us even when it is disguised
As tolerance

True intentions pierce the deceitful veil of
justice
When will we see the senselessness
In battle amongst brethren?
When will we begin to value the lives
Of those who disagree with us?

What a small and selfish world
We are a part of
A nation of crumbling values
A new stone of trust lost
To the infinite abyss of greed
With each passing hour
The world shifts on its axis

Perhaps someday when each of us
Is reduced to dust, we shall see
What foolishness we were a part of
We will see that there was no hero, nor villain
But rather, one maker
Sending wounded hearts into battle

"Fight" whispers the maker of the weapons
Who revels in his scheme
His greed grows
But his presence remains the same
In the shadows he stands, watching
As two men are burdened with the narrative
Of hero, and villain

Father of Mine

He didn't carry her
He didn't nurse her
But he is every bit as much a part of her as her
mother

Instead of teaching her textbooks
He taught her lessons
How to ride a bike, How to be a hard worker
How to lead by example

Some nights he was tired
And some days he was off at work with much on
his mind
Juggling thoughts that far exceeded the depths of
her small world
But even still, he was there
There was always a long car ride
And early morning trips to the donut shop
Or a daddy-daughter dance to make up for lost
time

It didn't matter that he didn't talk much
He tried his best to listen
And when there were no more words

There was music
Something else he passed down to her
Songs they both knew
A tune to absentmindedly hum to
With fingers tapping

And when there were too many words
In a world filled with talking
And lacking listening
She thought of him and his quiet ways
It's always the quiet people who are easiest to
talk to

He didn't carry her
He didn't nurse her
But he is every bit as much a part of her as her
mother

The Muse

What a fortunate curse
To be a writer with a pleasant muse
Someone who plays for me
Rather than inflicts on me
The blues
What a specific and splendid problem to have
The peace and quiet in my mind may proceed to
drive me mad
And for all the little hells I've been through
Something has come of it
A story, a poem, a creation, a reward

And now it seems this is the ultimate trade
Sad in and of itself that I've grown so
accustomed
To to being rewarded with something to write
about
By going through the unbearable

And now I have the gift of you
My sweet and tender
Gentle muse
Now the thoughts have slowed
Like the heartbeat of the decrepit and doomed

The words are a trickle where there once was an
ocean
But I'm not sorry and I'm not mad
What a wonderful, splendid problem to have

Wallflower

I'm Honored to be a wallflower
In your world of make-believe
Nothing more than a quiet observer
I never want to leave
I watch with wonder as the wonder of your mind
Pursues a happily ever after
In a place I'm yet to find
Maybe I'm so far removed
From the land of make-believe
That now my mind wanders only over dark
thoughts
And troubled seas
But oh to be a wallflower
In your world of make-believe
Maybe someday you'll take me back
I pray you never leave

If You Decide

For my child who I do not yet know
Some words for you as you grow
I promise to always hug you close
And hold you tight
To listen to you when the time is right… or
wrong
I promise to always tell you
How you are beautifully and wonderfully made
Colors of lovely in every shade
And if ever there's a time you don't feel the
same
That you decide to hate the way your tummy
looks
Or your legs, your eyes, your nooks- and
crannies
I will hold you still, and let you cry
Then my child, I'll look you in the eye
And tell you it's okay, at the end of the day
I love you enough for the both of us
A hundred times over
And I'm sorry for whatever it is that I said or did
To let you forget all that I'd give
So that you would know your worth
I'd apologize for the people who won't
For the media, the movies and even the books

That made you feel like you weren't
Enough, I vow, I could go on
But instead I think I'll hold you
I will not fight with you
I will not become cross
That would only be my loss
If you decide
You don't like your looks
Darling, I'll fill you with my love
As words fill pages in a book.

I Remember You

I was nine when you left
Then eleven twice
Then a few years for acceptance
But seventeen was not nice
The first time it happens
Shock and panic set in
But the darkness comes to conquer when
I'm all alone with my thoughts
Alone in your absence
And with this realization that
I've said my last words to you

And what did they mean?
It's never some grand soliloquy
It's never enough words
It counts for nothing
Because even though I got to know you for as
long as I did
And said every thought I could think out loud
There are still an infinite amount of things
unsaid

And time is cruel and it doesn't care
And I have and have always had so much to
share

But you're gone
You're not here
To hear
What I think or have to say
And I know that you would
If you had the time
If you had a day
I miss you
And I try to find the sound of your voice in the
breeze
In the colors of the sunsets
In the trees
I'll look for peace instead, I know you are free
But still I do not know what to do
When I'm lost and lonely and wanting for you
Your absence is as cold as the month of
December
So I do all that I can to try and remember
You
And I do some days more than others
I can almost hear your voice
I can almost feel your touch
How thankful I am for memories
That try their best to keep you alive
In my heart
In my mind
In the visions of my closed eyes
I remember you

Heavy

I know you are heavy my darling
I see it on your face
I hear it in your voice

It's as if the world has come crashing down on
you without warning
And peace is not a given on any given morning
Please hand me your weight, it was never yours
to bear
Don't trick yourself into letting it be something
you wear
A badge, a medal of honor
Because where do we go when we are pushed
farther
And farther apart?
The more of the world you hold in your hands
The less and less I see
Of the plan
This weight has consumed you
This weight is a lie
It has kept us both from feeling alive
And how could we?
Weight is suffocating and hard to take on
We are glass and this is the rock which we break
on

This won't be easy but please let us try
To lay our weight down and look to the sky
The world is not in our hands
The world is out there
The sun rises and sets
Life may never be fair
But it's here and we have it
Hold on while it lasts
Someday this weight will be a weight of the past

Old Friend

I'm sorry for how things had to end
I'm sorry yours was not a brokenness which I
could mend
And most importantly I'm sorry that you were in
my life for a mere season
In that time you gave me a reason
To learn and love and grow as I am
I'm sorry you had to hand
Me over to something new
We never thought that as we grew
We would in turn outgrow each other
Looking and looking for another
To fill the space
What a waste
Of time it was
To think people could be dispensable
The ink of their impact rinsable
We have written words on the walls of each
other's hearts
Exchanged secrets in whispers
Showed our burns and blisters
And that is not something that can be erased or
undone
I'm just sorry that it all has come
To an end

The end
We closed the book
And perhaps left some pages blank
But still there are days when I wake
Up
And am thankful for everything about our time
together
Because in the end I know
I learned from you
I'm sorry I had to turn from you
Old friend
I hope you are well
Old friend
It's still your soul to sell

Hello, Stranger

How frequently disregarded is the significance
of strangers
Hellos and goodbyes come and go
But goodbye is never really goodbye to us
Is it?
In our naivety we mistake goodbye for "see you
later"
Like an abandoned palette awaiting a painter
And the next hello for an eventuality.
How little we examine the reality
That we are promised next to nothing

Not a second chance
Not another glance
Another laugh, another dance
One more embrace
One more chance to see their face

We pass so many lives each day
But never do we stop to weigh
The significance of their heartbeat
Of their thoughts and words
We just assume that they're heard
By someone
Or no one

Who really cares?

And don't dare say that you do
Or that everyone does
They don't until it's too late
And life succumbs to fate
The toll of death refuses to wait
For you to find significance
In the life
Of a stranger
And that's the real danger
That we are all so numb to hellos and goodbyes
What will it take for us to open our eyes?

My Monster

And where are we supposed to go
To escape our own thoughts
Is it even possible?
We can run all we want
But the voices are in our heads
No more monsters under our beds

We can stand behind the curtains
Hide beneath the covers
But they still know where to find us
And when it all becomes too much
We drop down on our knees and beg
For mercy
From our minds
But our minds are us and we are them
I miss the monsters under my bed

The silence only makes their noises louder
Growling and clawing, thrashing like the
crashing waves
And there's no one here to come and save
Me

So where do we go

To escape ourselves?
How do we quiet the monsters?
And if silence isn't an option
How do we keep them caged?
Loud and hungry and enraged

The last thing I want to do
Is let my monsters scare you too
They are irrational and unavoidable
They will come after you

We took for granted
The monsters under our beds
As children not knowing
They'd soon be in our heads

Rage Above and Within

The sky is enraged
It screams and it cries
And still I find some peace in this
I feel for the sky
Oh why are you angry? Why are you hurt? Is it
my fault?
I question my worth
The rain is good
But what of the storm?
A buildup, a breakdown, a breakthrough
I'm torn
Louder, louder and louder still
The winds are weighted and the winds are strong
The clouds care not who they explode on
Their only concern is letting go to move on

Letting go of their weight and their sobs and
cries
Tears of hot and cold fall from the skies

And what torture to know that the sky will still
break

No matter what I do
I will not have what it takes
I cannot fix the sky
I cannot stop it from its raging cry
But I can sit in the rain
Share in the pain
Let the tears wash away together
Watch the puddles form on the ground
Water rising higher and higher until the sky
Has no more tears to cry
The gray subsides
The sun will rise
And the sky is blue again
You feel like you again

Messed Up

How easily praise turns into accidental pride
We preach humility from the blind corner of our
eye
Like a car we do not want to steer
We find it hard to look in the mirror
Because we know exactly what we'll see
An image of hypocrisy staring back at me
The ground could shake and the earth quake
And still our first thought would be "but what
about me"
Surely everyone was watching me as buildings
were falling
As people were screaming for help
Because the world revolves around the
perception of me
The mirage of my humility
And dedication
The more and more I think about this situation
I realize
I'm messed up
We're all so deeply messed up
Even the things that are sacred and good
Are not safe from our false pride and misplaced
prejudices

Perhaps it is true that we have failed ourselves
and each other
We do not call on each other often enough
We do not admit our pride for fear that
We will be treated as anomalies
We're all so full of it
This pride
Our humanity warping our morality
I cannot stand on a pedestal any more than you
We cannot separate the black and the blue
These bruises on our ego that we hide so well
These things that we think but wouldn't dare to
tell
But maybe we can turn this around
Maybe it starts in you and me and spreads
throughout a town
A city, a state, a nation
Look up, look at yourself, do not look down
On people around you
The problem started with people like me and
you
Perhaps if we're lucky, it ends with us too

Bloody Knees

If you fall and scrape your knee
Is your blood less red than that
Which came from tumbling out of the tree?
Or perhaps the blood of a worker bee

If you walk in the rain with an umbrella and coat
Are the clouds above you raining less
Than those above the unsheltered goat?

No?

So then you surely must see
What's true for you is not true for me
Or them or him or her
But still our lives pass by in a blur
Of selfishness and seldom with the realization
That someone else's life
Is not a vacation
Or an invitation
For comparison

Your experiences are not less than
Your experiences are not more
They are simply experiences
Keep your wandering eye away from the lure

The draw, the temptation
To second guess
To run from rest
To lie to yourself that there is always more
You are so busy
You're making me dizzy

Slow down, dear friend
Sit down so I have time to mend
Your scraped up knee

To a child
A kiss can help as much as a band-aid
I thought of this as I laid
Down
Down with my head, my worried head
I'm not broken, I'm just hurt
Someone tell me, tell me my worth

You don't have to shatter to be broken
You don't have to be broken to be hurt
You don't have to be more hurt than me to need
help
You don't have to hurt to have worth
Let me lend you my umbrella
Stand with me and my blood soaked knee
We will rest together

Noise

Shake the ground

Make a sound
For God's sake did you forget how to be loud?
Where is your voice?
You have a choice
Make a sound
Make a sound
Do not fade into the background
I wish you were loud
I feel so small and quiet and voiceless
I hate that I live in the noisiest noise-less world
Everyone is talking so no one is listening
What if we all just took turns?
Would that turn
Anything around?
Or are we too far gone?
Our sense of kindness
Our ability to listen
Six dark feet under the ground
Make a sound
Shake the ground

Not For Me

Mourn
But not for me
Cry and scream deafening cries
Get mad at the world
Get mad at they whys
Something good inside me dies
Mourn
On your knees
At your bedside
Mourn
But not for me
I have no reason left to hide
I've yelled at the world for far too long
I see no reason to go on with this
Woe is me
No
Woe to the world for its dissonance
And for its disbelief in tenderness
Mourn
For the lost and for the broken
Mourn
But not for me
I'm just one person and I'm mostly okay
But mourn for those who have no one left to
mourn them

Or what they had to say
Mourn for the ways of the leaders
Who don't have a clue
Who can't take a hint from me or from you
Now I
Pass down the crown
The grieving of humility, humanity
Do you see?
Do you see?
Listen
And look
And feel what you feel
Say what you think but not for me
Mourn
But not for me